Carving Santas for Today
with Tom Wolfe

Tom Wolfe

4880 Lower Valley Road, Atglen, Pa 19310

Other Schiffer Books by Tom Wolfe

Santa and His Friends: Carving with Tom Wolfe. Size: 8 1/2" x 11" ■ 250+ color photos ■ 64 pp. ■ ISBN: 0-88740-277-1 ■ soft cover ■ $9.95

Santimals: Carving with Tom Wolfe. Tom Wolfe. Size: 8 1/2" x 11" ■ 280 color photos ■ 64 pp. ■ ISBN: 0-88740-440-5 ■ soft cover ■ $12.95

Tom Wolfe Carves Jointed Santas. Tom Wolfe. Size: 8 1/2" x 11" ■ 300 color photos, patterns ■ 64 pp. ■ ISBN: 0-88740-539-8 ■ soft cover ■ $12.95

Traditional Santa Carving with Tom Wolfe. Size: 8 1/2" x 11" ■ 280 color photos ■ 64 pp. ■ ISBN: 0-88740-366-2 ■ soft cover ■ $12.95

More Santa Carving with Tom Wolfe. Size: 8 1/2" x 11" ■ 190 color photos ■ 64 pp. ■ ISBN: 0-7643-0626-X ■ soft cover ■ $14.95

Power Carving Santas with Tom Wolfe. Size: 8 1/2" x 11" ■ 260+ color photos, 16 patterns ■ 64 pp. ■ ISBN: 0-88740-963-6 ■ soft cover ■ $12.95

The Tom Wolfe Treasury: 75 Santa Patterns. Size: 8 1/2" x 11" ■ 75 patterns ■ 64 pp. ■ ISBN: 0-7643-0627-8 ■ soft cover ■ $12.95

Schiffer Books are available at special discounts for bulk purchases for sales promotions or premiums. Special editions, including personalized covers, corporate imprints, and excerpts can be created in large quantities for special needs. For more information contact the publisher:

Published by Schiffer Publishing Ltd.
4880 Lower Valley Road
Atglen, PA 19310
Phone: (610) 593-1777; Fax: (610) 593-2002
E-mail: Info@schifferbooks.com

For the largest selection of fine reference books on this and related subjects, please visit our web site at
www.schifferbooks.com
We are always looking for people to write books on new and related subjects. If you have an idea for a book please contact us at the above address.

This book may be purchased from the publisher.
Include $3.95 for shipping.
Please try your bookstore first.
You may write for a free catalog.

In Europe, Schiffer books are distributed by
Bushwood Books
6 Marksbury Ave.
Kew Gardens
Surrey TW9 4JF England
Phone: 44 (0) 20 8392-8585; Fax: 44 (0) 20 8392-9876
E-mail: info@bushwoodbooks.co.uk
Website: www.bushwoodbooks.co.uk
Free postage in the U.K., Europe; air mail at cost.

Copyright © 2008 by Tom Wolfe
Library of Congress Control Number: 2008925417

All rights reserved. No part of this work may be reproduced or used in any form or by any means—graphic, electronic, or mechanical, including photocopying or information storage and retrieval systems—without written permission from the publisher.
The scanning, uploading and distribution of this book or any part thereof via the Internet or via any other means without the permission of the publisher is illegal and punishable by law. Please purchase only authorized editions and do not participate in or encourage the electronic piracy of copyrighted materials.
"Schiffer," "Schiffer Publishing Ltd. & Design," and the "Design of pen and ink well" are registered trademarks of Schiffer Publishing Ltd.

Designed by RoS
Type set in Zurich BT

ISBN: 978-0-7643-3082-7
Printed in China

Introduction

I am amazed that, of all the things I carve, Santa Claus has always brought the greatest interest. Maybe it is because this "jolly old elf" can take on so many forms and attitudes. I've made tall Santas and short ones, skinny and fat, serious and comical. I've dressed them in red suits, blue suits, and plaid suits; long robes, blue jeans, and Bermuda shorts. They have been full-figures and busts, ornaments, canes, and bottle stoppers.

But whatever the incarnation, whatever shape or form, the Santa spirit seems to break through. There is something joyful, nostalgic, loving, and fanciful about him, and it is this appeal that keeps carvers coming back again and again.

So here is yet another Santa carving book. Here he is walking at a jaunty pace with cane in hand. Perhaps he is on the way to the workshop to see how preparations are proceeding or on the way to the stable to check on the reindeer. There is a look of anticipation in his face.

As always I have tried to produce a book that can be used for carvers at all levels of experience. For the new carver there are step-by-step, illustrated instructions for moving from a block of wood to the finished work. For the more experienced carver there are some new techniques and details that will help make their carving experience more enjoyable and productive.

I have also included a large gallery of recent Santas created using this method. You will see how it lends itself to a wide variety of figures and forms. The only limit is the limitation of your imagination!

I hope you enjoy this book as much as I enjoyed putting it together.

The size of the block doesn't matter as long as the ends are square. Any length can be used, each giving a different character to the Santa.

This carving will begin with the cap. Determine the position of the shoulder.

Move up a little and cut a stop to define the top of the tassel of the cap on one corner.

Cut back to the stop from above.

Do the same on the bottom edge of the tassel. Cut a stop…

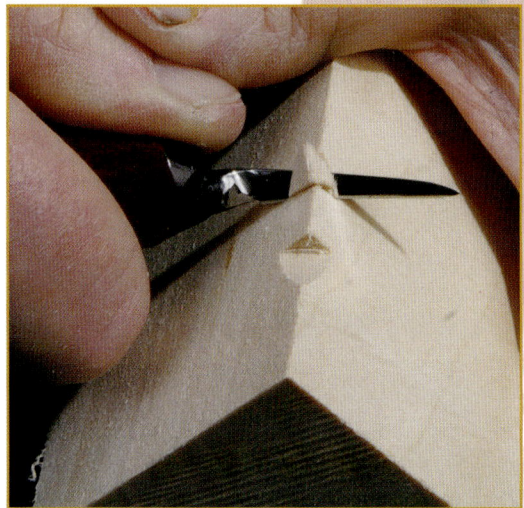

…and trim back to it.

The result.

Make a stop on the side of the tassel.

Trim back with a scoop cut, first from one direction…

…then the other. This piece should pop out.

The result.

Knock off the four corners of the tassel…

...taking it to an octagonal shape.

Progress.

Next round off the tassel. By going through the octagonal stage it is much easier to get spots like this truly round.

Progress.

With the tassel formed we can work on the cap. The area above the tassel is the folded-over part of the cap. Flatten it down. Start on the edge of the block...

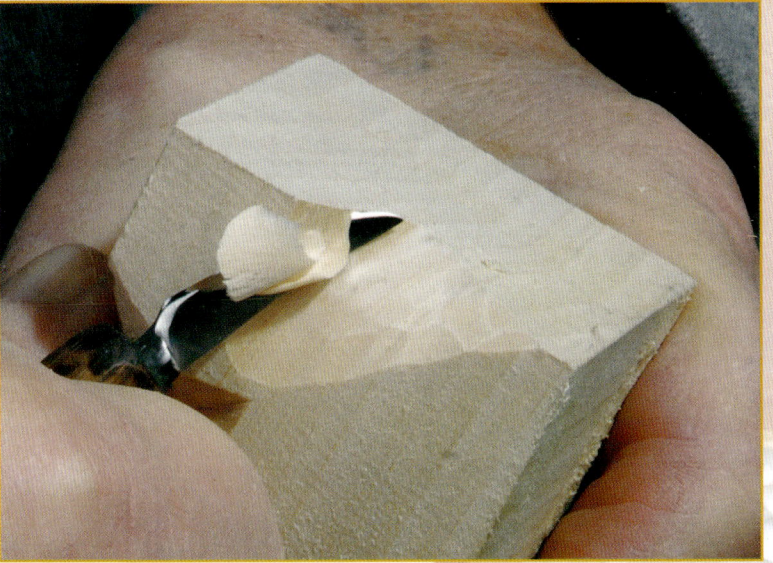
...and gradually scoop down to the cap.

Continue around the folded over part of the cap.

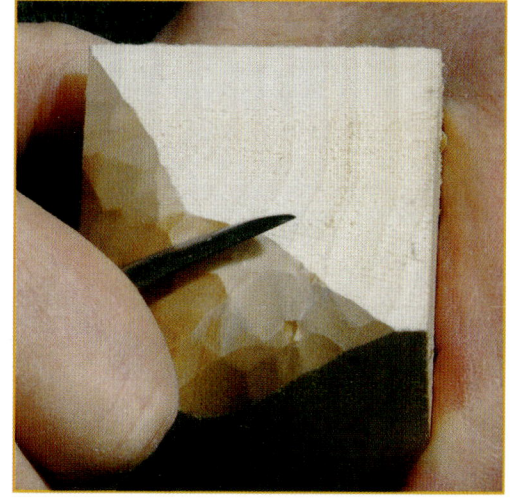

Carve to the diagonal midpoint of the block end.

Progress.

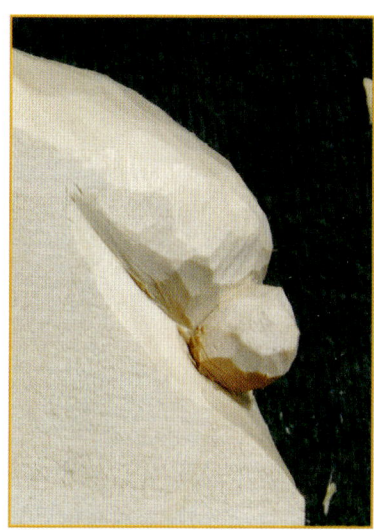

Now do about the same thing from the other side...

...making kind of a "roof."

Progress.

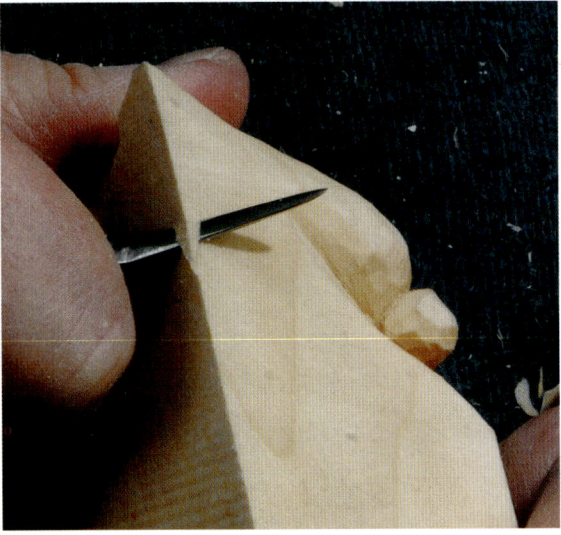

The nose will be on a corner edge of the block. Visualize the nose and knock off the corner edge, working up from the tip of the nose.

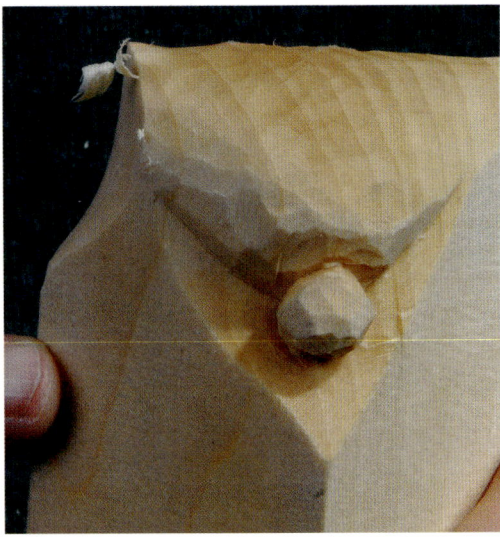

The result is this scoop cut.

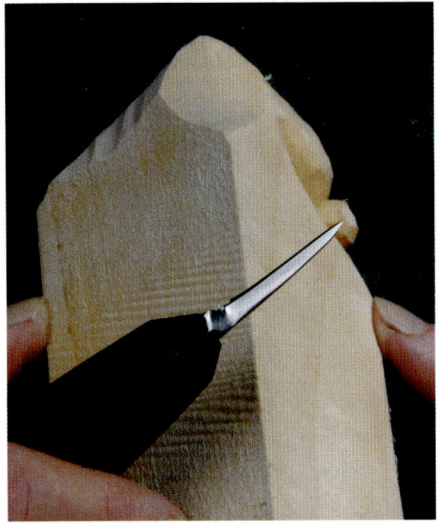

Determine the overall length of the head. Line up the other shoulder opposite the tassel.

On that edge, trim up from the shoulder to help define the head.

The result.

Now that we have defined the shoulder, we can set the hairline. Starting a little bit above the shoulder line, trim the back corner of the head.

You are trying to establish the depth of the head, so remove wood from the back and the front...

...until you get the thickness you want. This defines the depth of the head and its overall size. The back of the head comes down to the neck line (at the left), and the front to the nose (at the right).

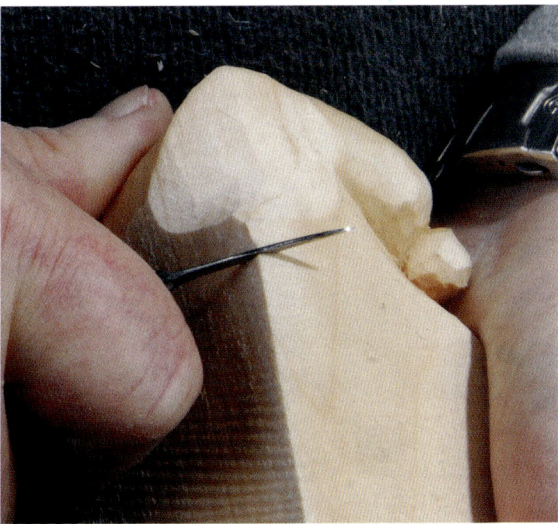

Cut a stop at the bottom of the nose.

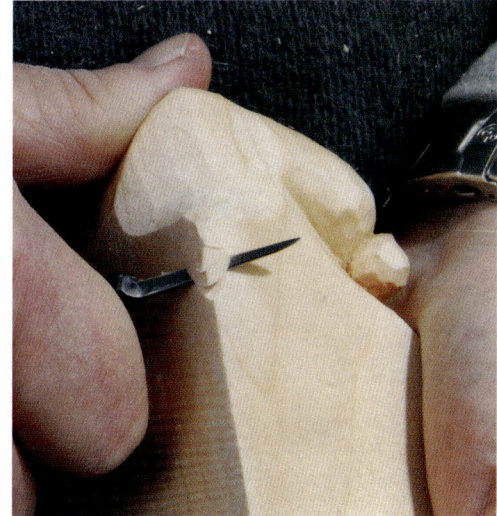

Trim back from the lip.

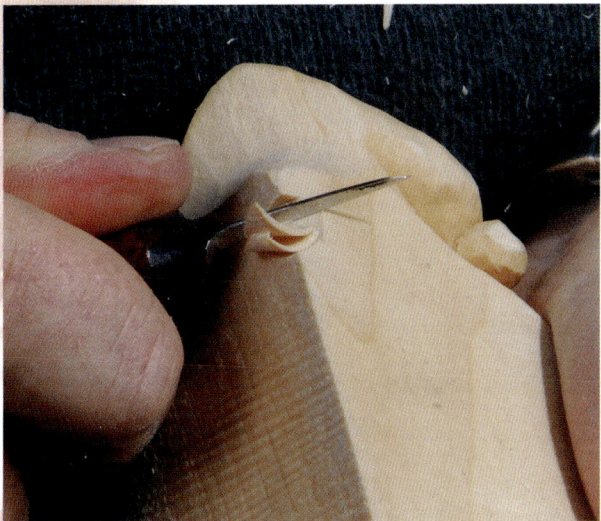

The cut needs to be repeated so it is quite deep, looking more like a beak than a nose for now.

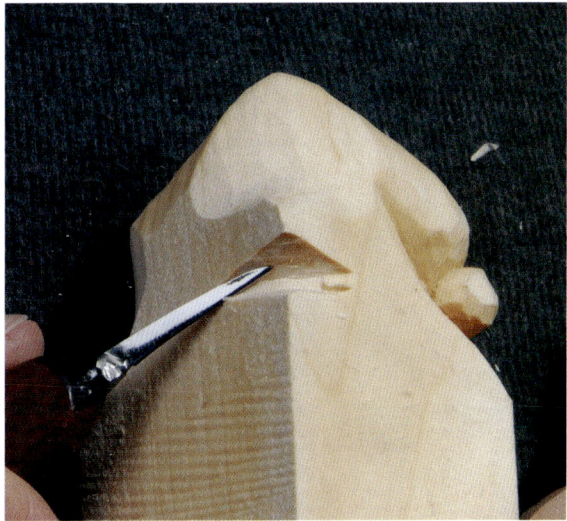

Progress.

Cut an angled stop at the nostril, going back to the cheek.

Trim back to the stop from the upper lip.

This ridge beside the nose has to go. Cut a stop along the nose...

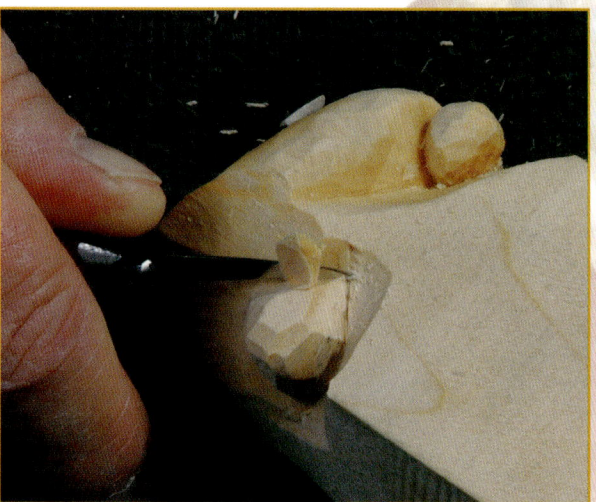
...and trim back to it from the cheek.

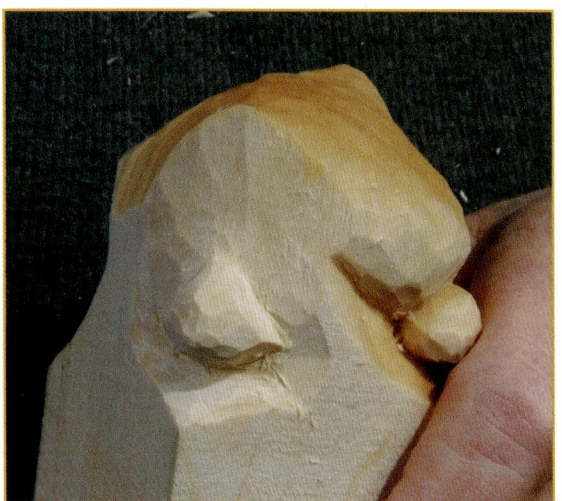
Progress.

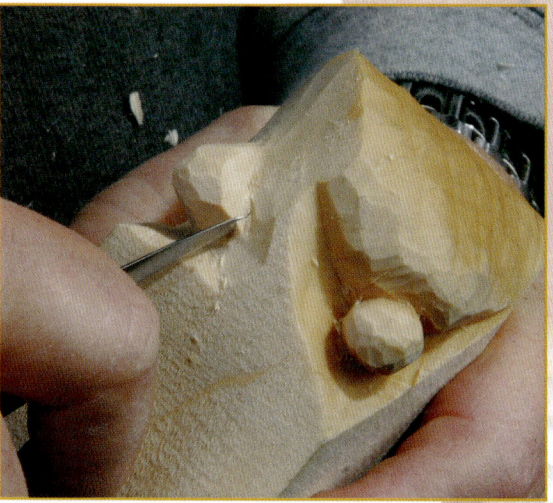
The smile line is created with a stop at the back of the nostril...

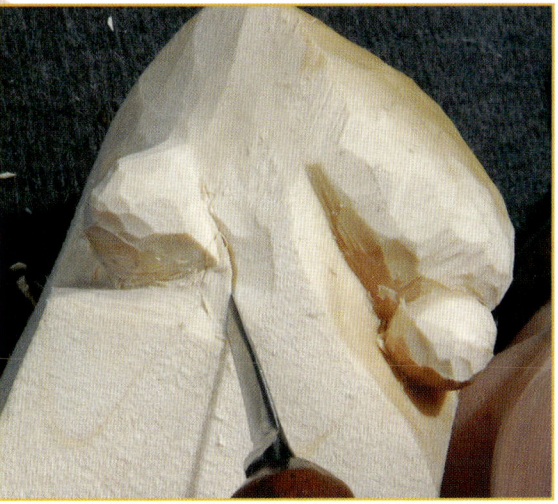
...another along the smile line of the cheek.

Trim back along the surface of the upper lip and the piece will pop out.

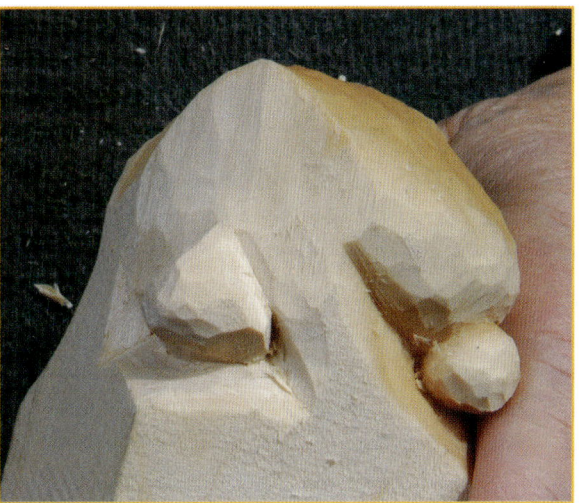
Progress.

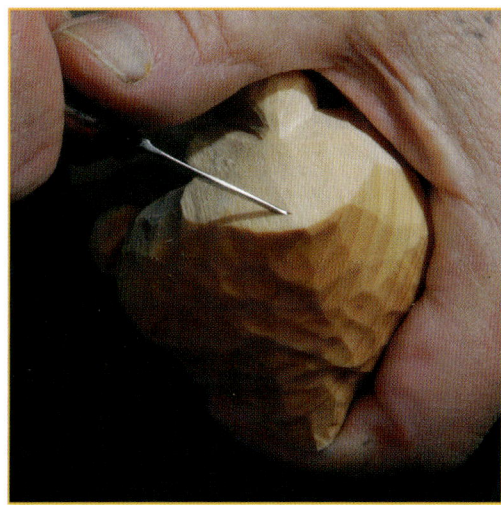
The foldover is made by plunging the knife in on one side...

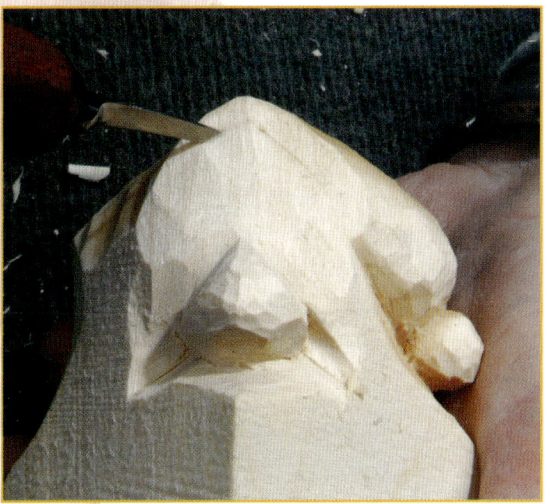
...and the other to create sort of a gable.

Trim it out with a straight cut underneath from the forehead.

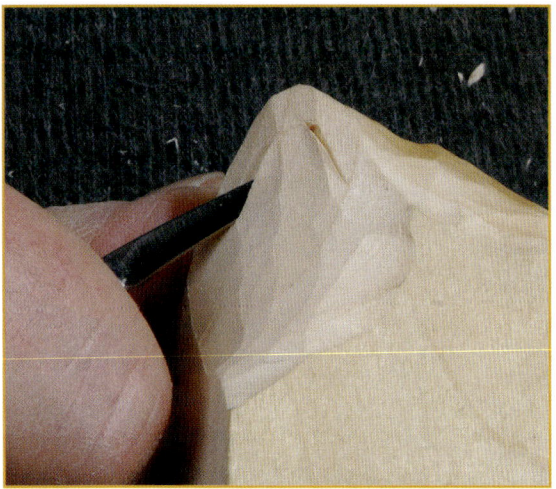
Repeat the process in the back. Cut the gable.

Trim underneath.

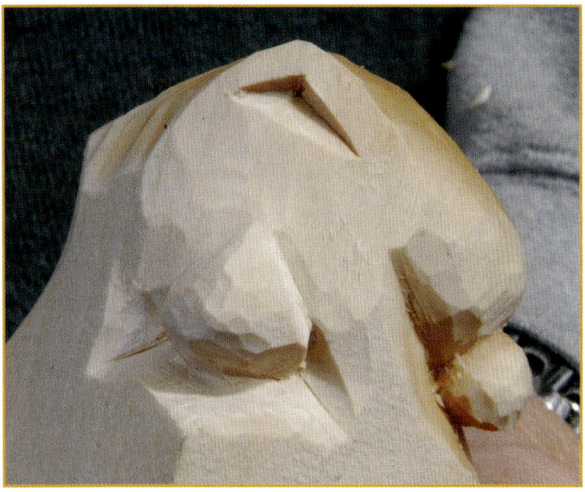
Progress.

Carry the line down using the knife...

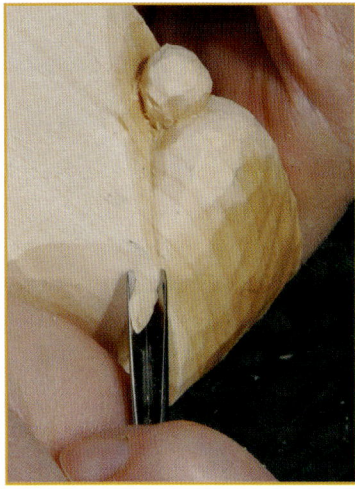
...or a gouge

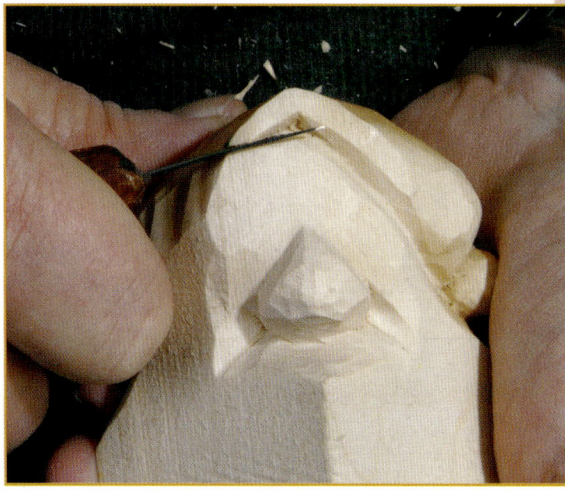
Start the top line of the cap's fur trim, front...

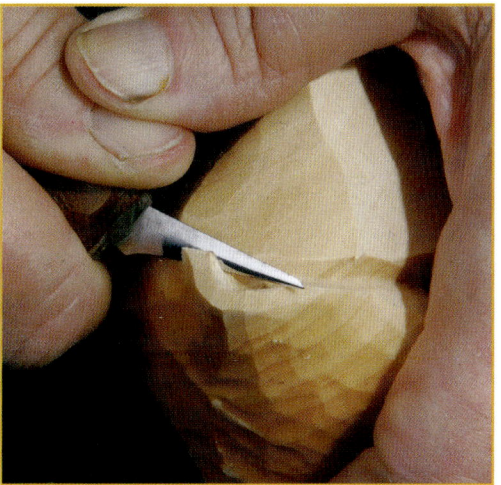

...and back.

Mark the line between the two points. This will help keep it level.

Follow the line with a v-tool.

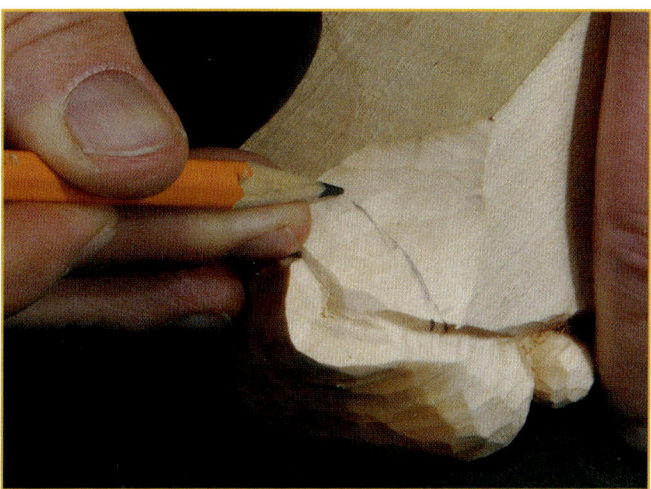

Determine the thickness of the fur trim and, running your finger in the upper edge groove as a depth gauge, mark the lower edge of the fur trim.

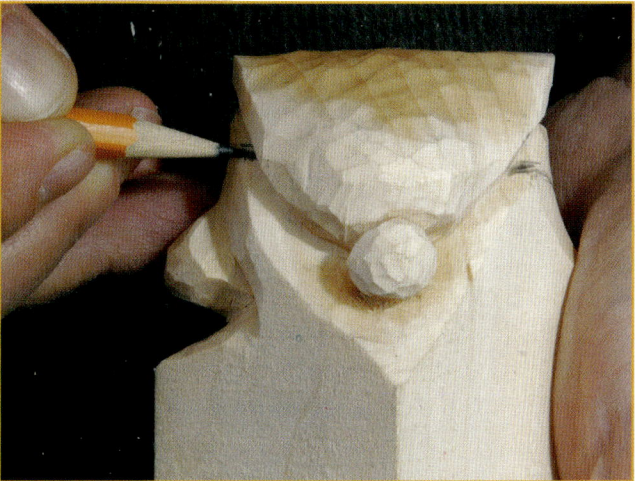

Make sure the marks align where they go under the foldover.

Use the v-tool again to cut the lower edge.

With a gouge carve out from the bridge of the nose to create space for the eyes.

Progress. A lot of character is carried by the eyes. Here I have made one eye lower than the other.

Draw the hairline on the tassel side of the hat.

Progress.

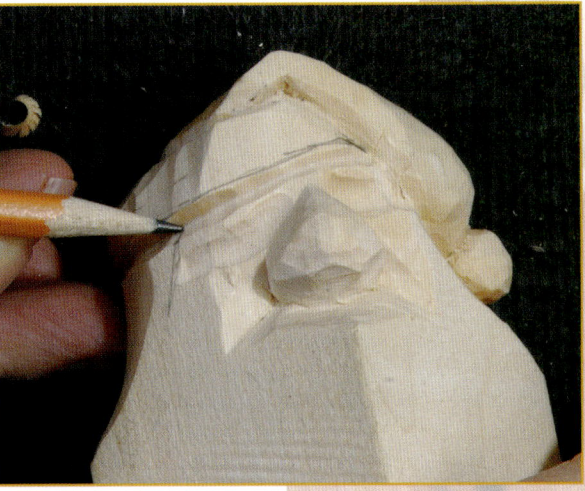
By looking down on the head, you can match the hairline when drawing the other side.

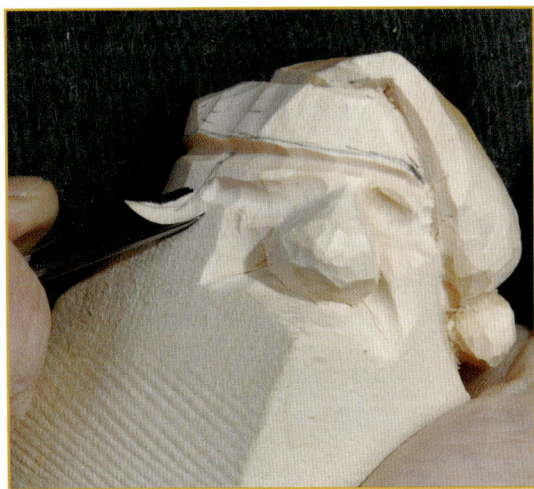
Use the v-tool to define the hairline.

Carry the line around the back.

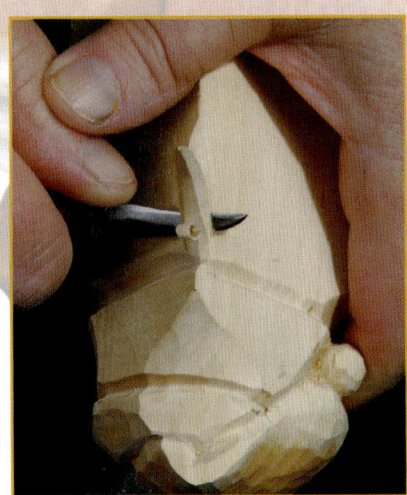
At the back, trim the corner of the block to the hairline.

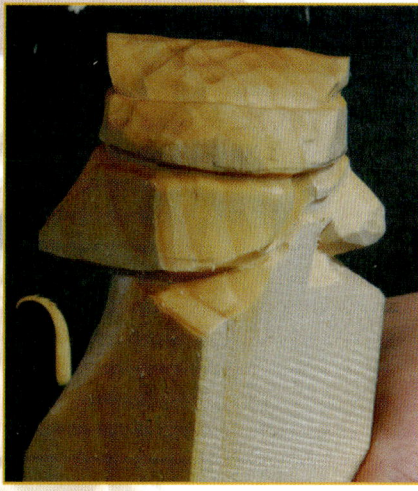
This will go deep, about halfway to the shoulders.

Carve the slope of the shoulders toward the hairline. Make several cuts…

…then trim them off under the hairline.

Progress.

Draw in the line of the beard.

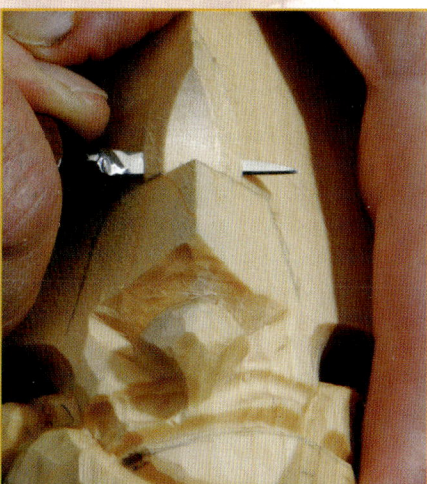
Cut a stop in the bottom of the beard line and carve back to it from the chest.

Progress.

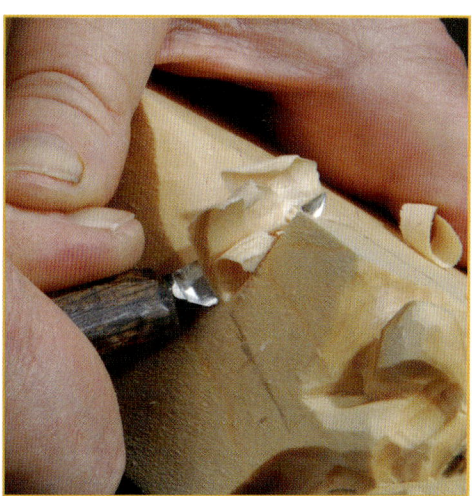
Continue the trimming down to flatten the chest area.

Progress. Now I'll turn my attention to the feet.

The wedge above the feet will be similar to that of the upper chest and quite deep.

Make a stop...

...and cut back to it.

Trim off the "feathers" and repeat the process.

Progress. The corners are deep enough, but the middle needs some more work.

Draw in the bottom of the coat. Again, fingers running along the bottom edge of the block make for a good depth gauge.

Use the same technique to draw the arm on one side…

…and the other.

Draw in the back of the knee.

Instead of a stop cut and trim, I carve this in both directions toward the middle…

…creating a valley.

Begin defining the front of the shoulder by cutting a stop along the outline of the beard...

...and trimming back to along the upper chest.

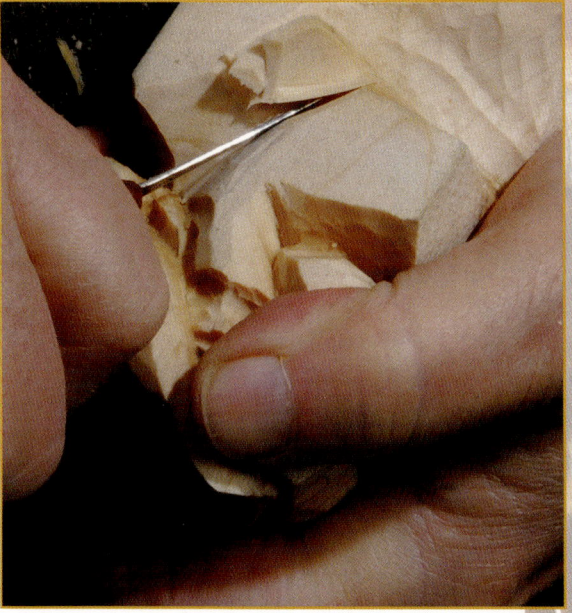

The surface will join the rest of the chest.

Progress.

Shape the beard some as you go.

The front of the beard is trimmed up into the area of the mustache.

The result.

The area of the mouth is created with two straight-in cuts into the mustache…

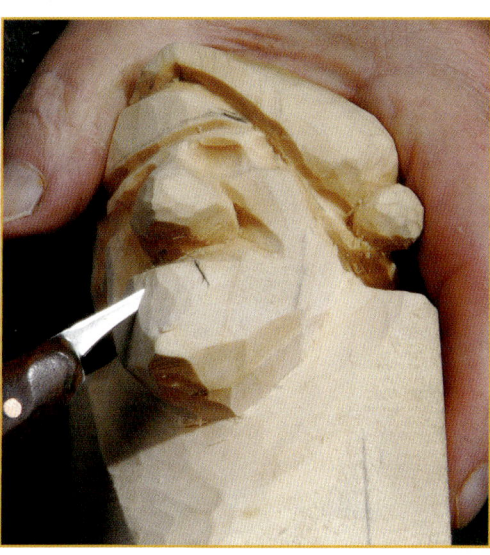
…one on either side, creating a triangle under the nose, where the mustache divides.

Cut across the bottom lip and pop out the area of the mouth.

This inverted pyramid shape is the result.

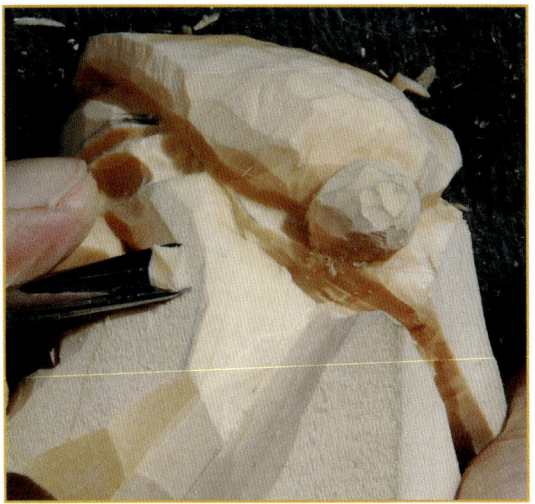

Gouge around the bottom of the cheek...

...coming in at the sideburn.

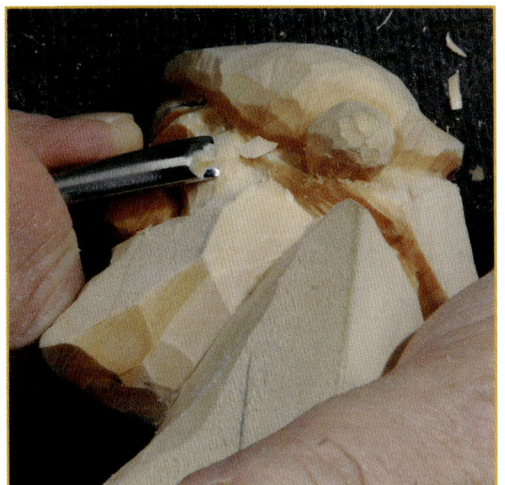

A #5 gouge rounds off the cheek.

Progress.

Make any adjustments necessary. Here I am deepening the lower cheek to bring out the mustache and balance the face.

Cut a stop in the lower edge of the moustache. It should be at the same angle as the eyebrows.

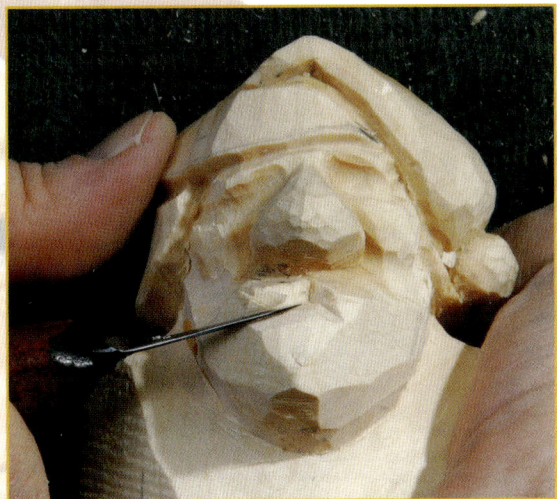
Trim back to it from the beard.

Mark the width of the mustache, where it will curl up at the ends.

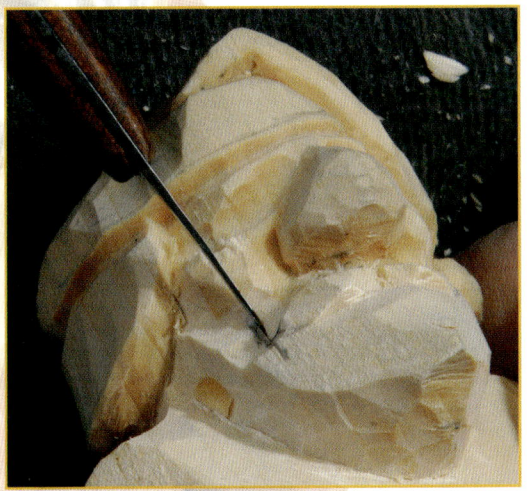
Make a stop on that line…

…cut back to it from the beard…

…and down from the cheek.

The result.

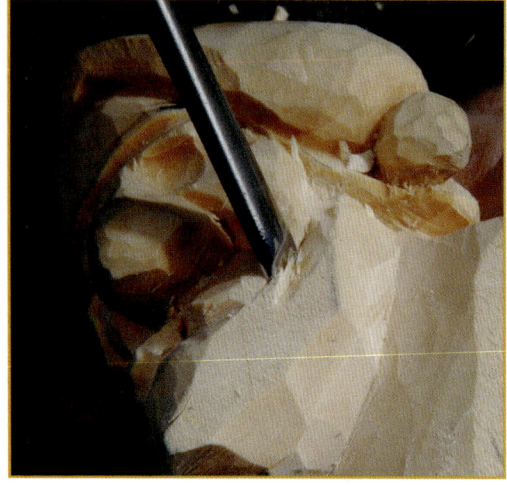
Press in on the mustache line with a gouge...

...and trim back to it from the beard.

Progress.

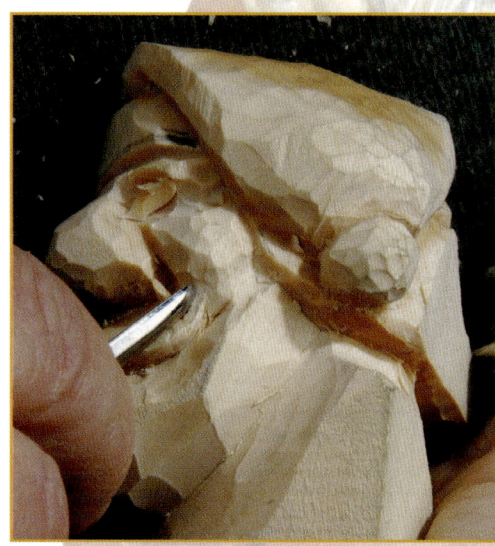
On the top of the mustache, push in with a #9 gouge to form the curl.

Repeat on the other side.

Trim back to it from the cheek.

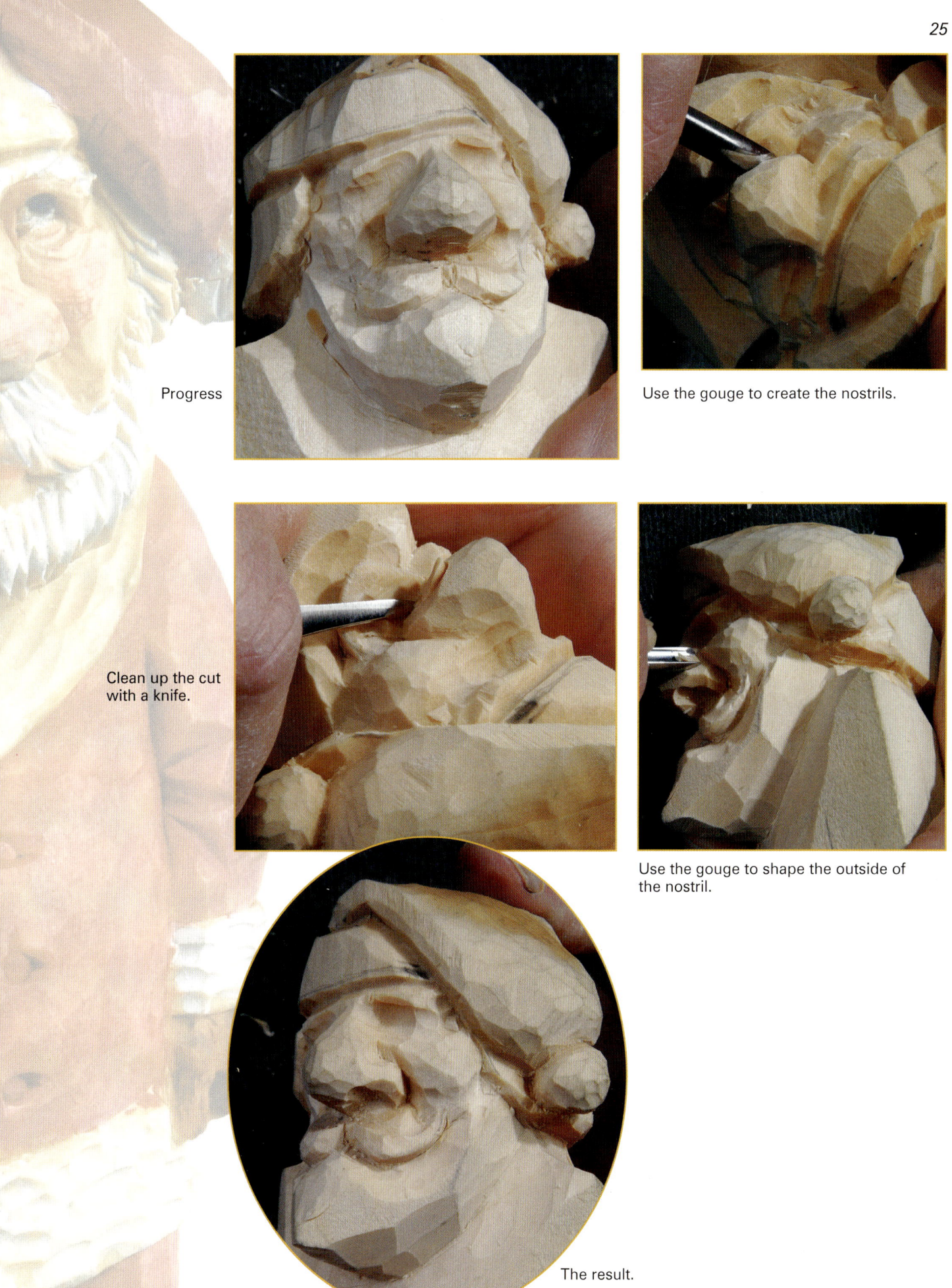

Progress

Use the gouge to create the nostrils.

Clean up the cut with a knife.

Use the gouge to shape the outside of the nostril.

The result.

25

Use a spoon gouge to shape the nose, make the tip more bulbous.

Use a gouge to separate the eyebrows.

Progress

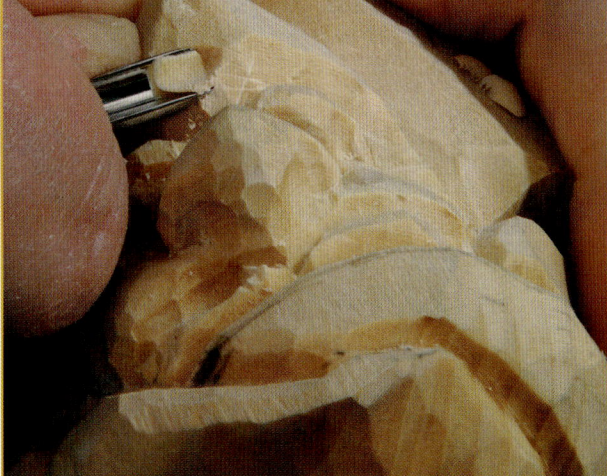

Using a gouge, go across the beard under the bottom lip. This will bring it out.

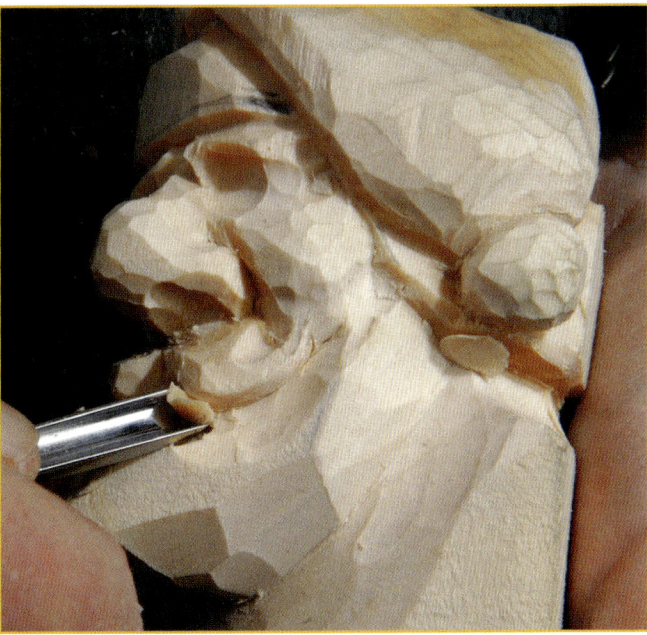

With the same tool turn the lower lip into the moustache.

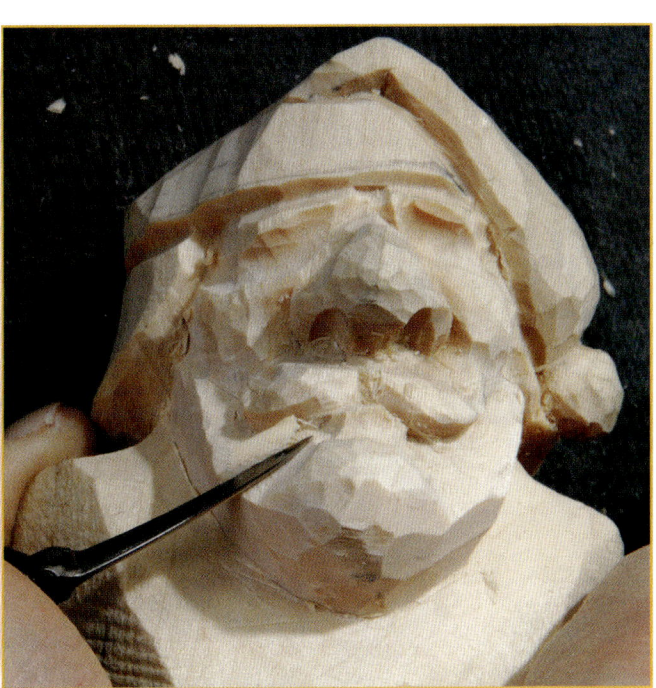

Shaping the beard under the corners of the mouth gives form to the beard, bringing out the chin.

Continue to shape the beard.

Returning to the coat, knock off some of the belly. Do the same on the back.

On the corners of the coat trim, make a stop…

…and trim back to it from the legs.

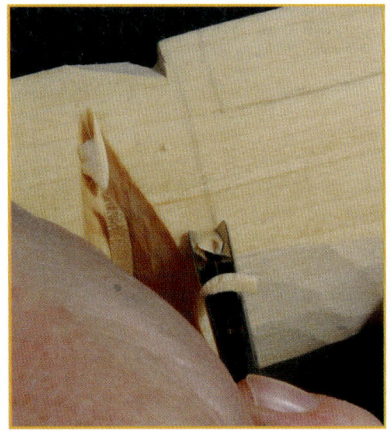

Follow the coat's hem line with a v-tool.

Use that line as a stop for trimming the legs.

To size the feet, begin with a center line on the base, from front to back.

Mark of the heel…

…and the toe.

Draw the back foot, making it a good size.

The other foot will be forward some. To keep it the same size use your fingers as a gauge…

…and transfer the length of the foot.

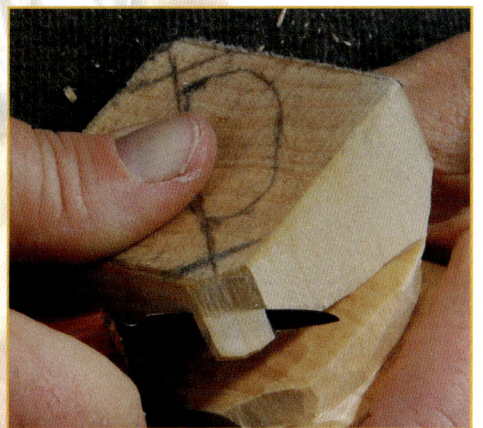
Trim the base to the back heel.

Make a deep stop to separate the feet.

Trim the heel of the forward foot to the stop.

Do the same thing at the toes.

Progress.

Trim the outside to the outline of the feet.

Progress.

Draw in the top of the right foot.

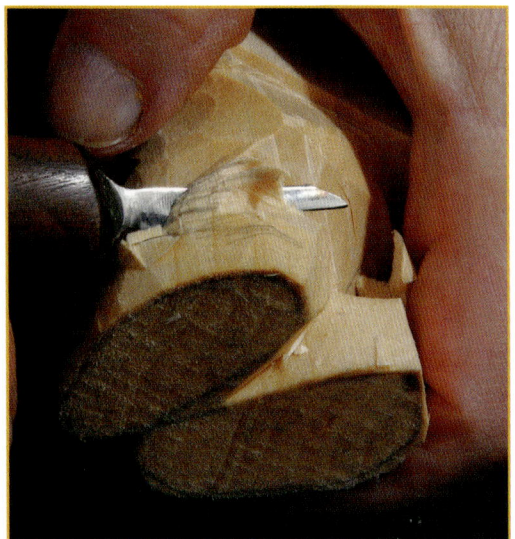
Carve out the area above the foot.

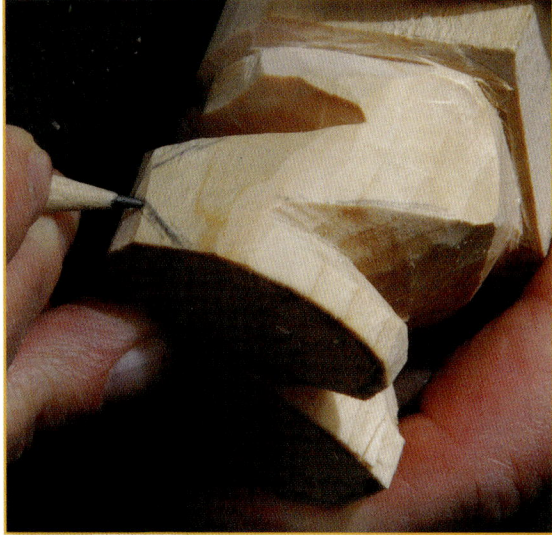
The right heel is lifted up a bit to give some movement to Santa. Mark it…

…and clip it off.

Thin the right leg so it looks like its coming from under the coat and right on down.

Beginning to look like a leg.

Use your pencil to mark what is to be removed from the left leg.

Carve it away.

Trim under the coat.

I want to separate the legs so that daylight shows through. Begin working at the area with a v-tool. Alternate carving from the front and from the back.

When you've worked your way through, you can begin to shape the legs.

Progress.

Before I forget I need to trim the sole at the front of the left foot. This will give it more of a walking look, and goes with the trimming we did to the heel on the right foot.

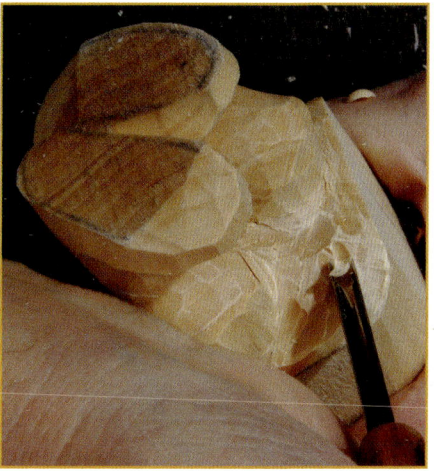
Use a gouge to undercut the coat.

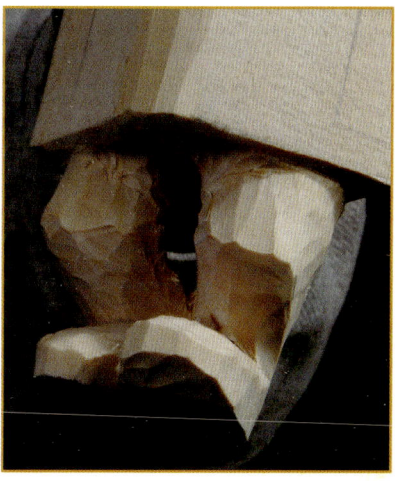
Extend this into the space between the legs. Opening these up higher makes the legs seem strong and less stubby.

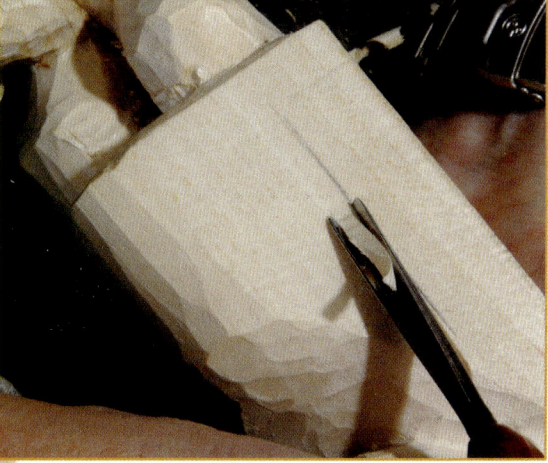
Use a v-tool to cut the arms away from the body, following the lines, front and back.

The arms were a bit long, so I'll take off a 1/2" or so.

Round the edge of the coat where the arms were.

Shape the back. Here I am using a gouge, working from the back of the arm. I want to remove enough to get rid of the stooped shoulder look.

Progress. The lower back is still full.

Moving to the front, I want to narrow the upper chest so I can bring the shoulder in a lot more.

Now I can give some shape to the lower back.

Progress to the coat

Mark the position of the hands.

Start at about the elbow and knock some off the shoulder.

Progress.

The top of the shoulders needs to be trimmed to the neck.

The head seems a bit wide. I will probably end up narrowing it by a 1/4 or 1/2 inch. I'm starting here under the fur trim of the cap, because it will allow me to see better what adjustments need to be made.

I'll narrow the face, too, probably by about this much.

To accomplish this I make a stop along the edge of the hat and sideburn...

...and cut back to it with the gouge.

Using a #9 gouge, carry the eye socket back to the temple.

Things domino. After I narrow the outside of the face, I will need to narrow the nose and cheeks. Then the face will probably look too long and I'll have to make more adjustments. Stay open to new possibilities as you carve!!!

Progress. Now I need to shorten the beard area so the face doesn't look so long.

The beard trimmed.

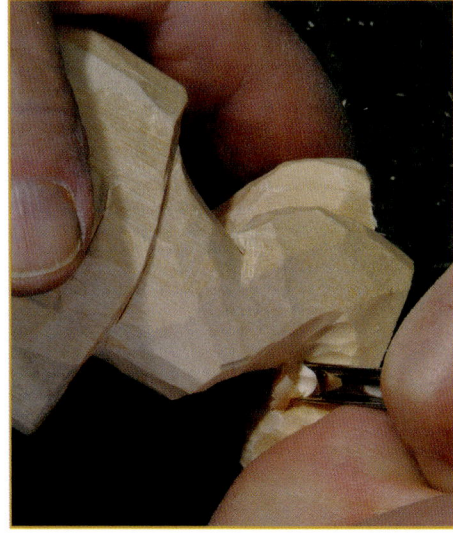

Another thick spot is the foot. It needs more work, including the shaping and narrowing of the instep.

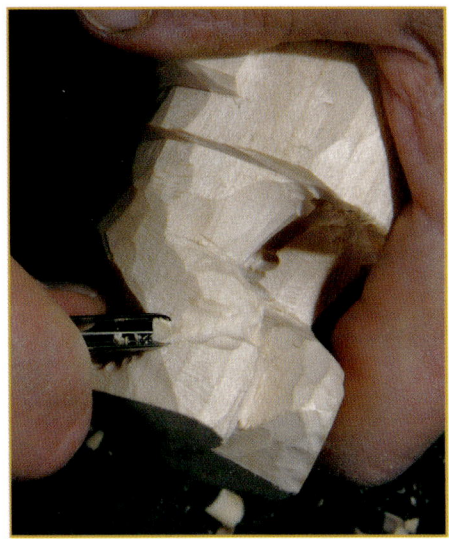

Narrow down the ankle as well.

The result.

gh as possible with-
ees. Make a stop cut

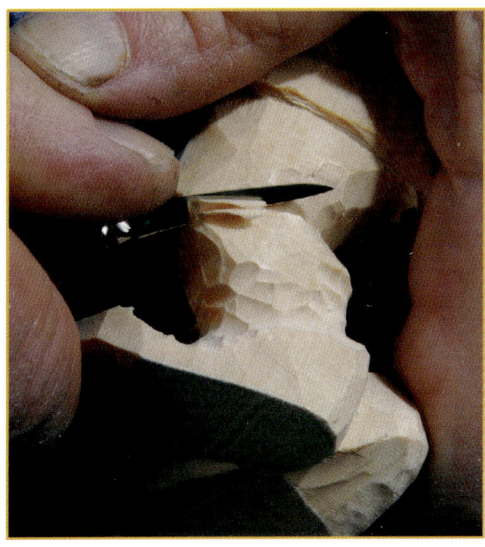
Trim back to it from the leg.

Cu

Trim back to it from the sole

The result.

At the bending points of the boot we need some accordion folds. These are simple slices. Cut one way…

...then the other.

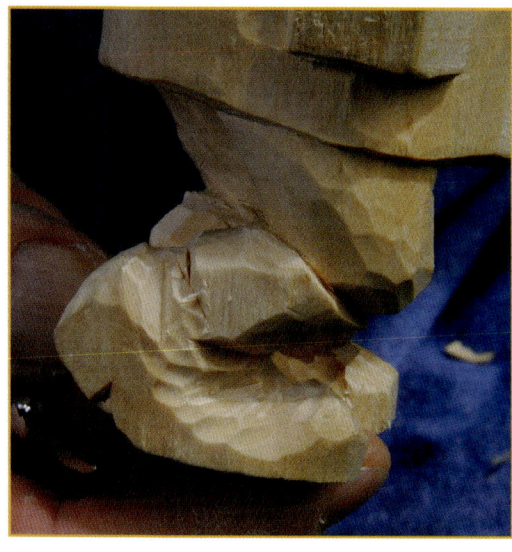
The result...

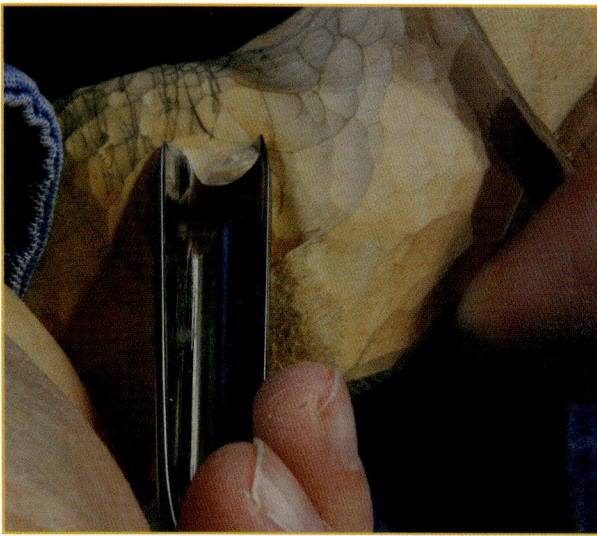
Work on the coat continues with the reduction of the rump.

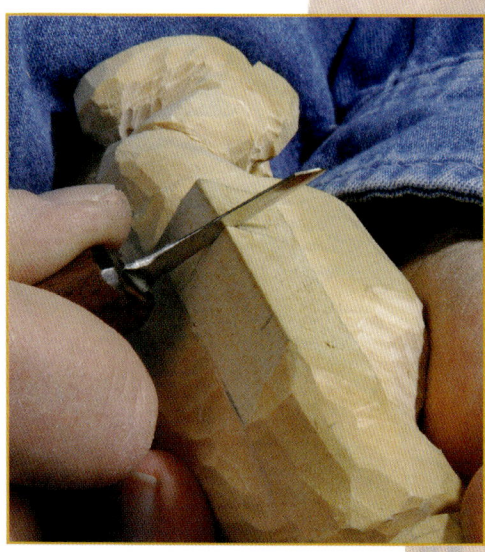
Make a stop at the end of the sleeve...

...and trim back to it from the mitten.

The hands blocked out.

Knock off the corner of the arm.

At the inside elbow, add folds to the front of the sleeve. I make three slices…one up…

…one down…

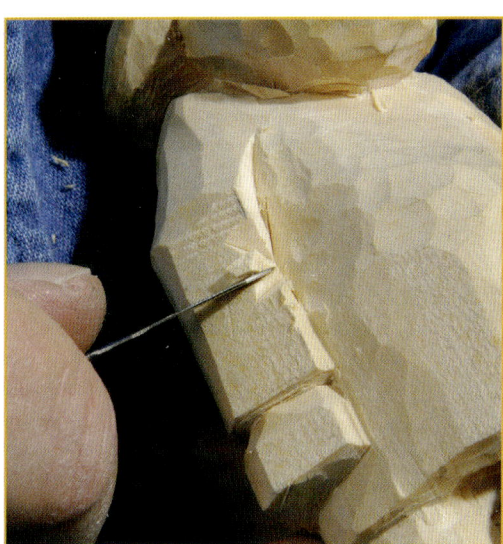

…and one in the middle.

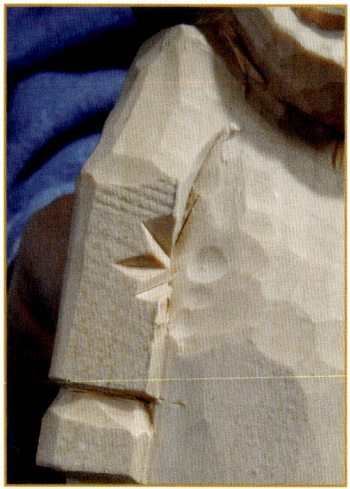

The result.

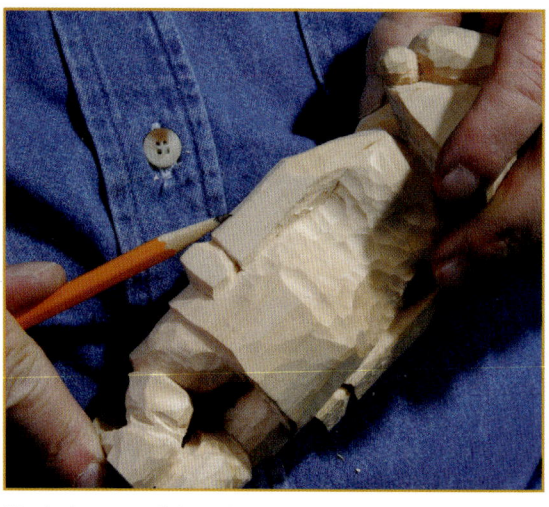

Mark the top of the trim on the sleeves. Again, I am using my forefinger to measure from the bottom of the foot so I can make the two sleeves equal.

Mark the fur at the bottom of the coat and at the collar.

Cut out a wedge at the opening of the collar.

Cut a stop in the opening and trim back to it from the other side.

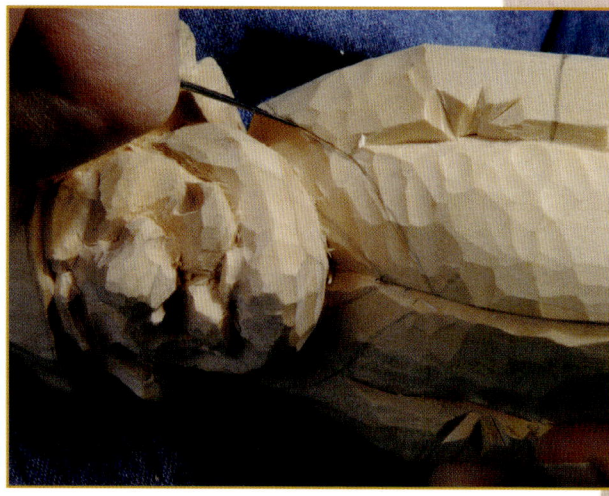

Make a stop around the collar...

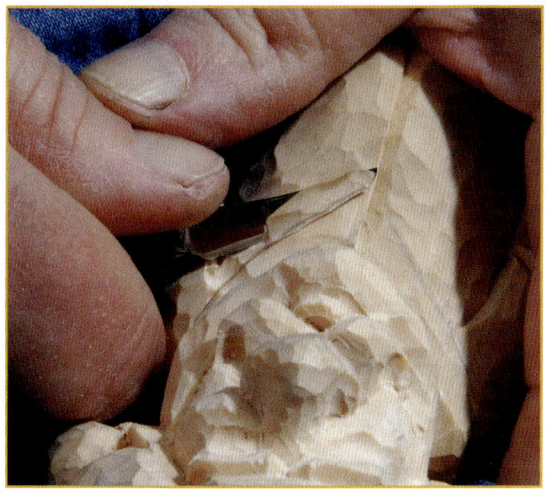
...and trim back to it from the coat.

Progress.

Use a v-tool to follow the fur trim line.

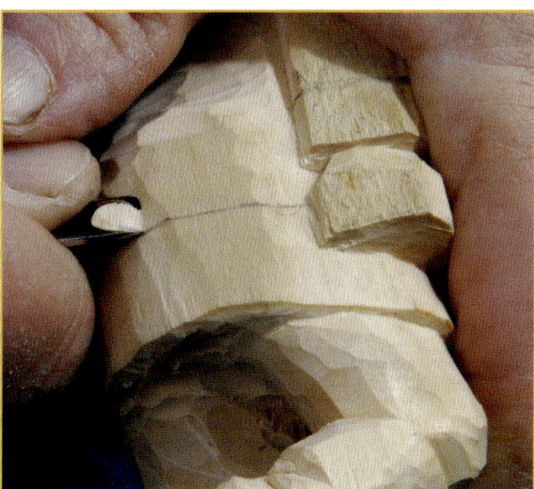
Trim back to the line to shape the coat.

Do the same thing on the trim of the sleeve.

The body is ready except for some detail work.

 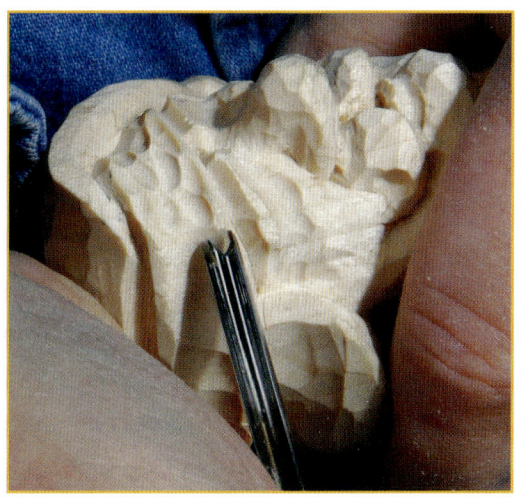

We'll start with the head. Run a gouge around the trim, going across the middle to give it cupped shape.

Give the trim texture by taking little nips with a small gouge. This will give a contrasting look to the hair and beard. Use the same method for the collar and trim.

 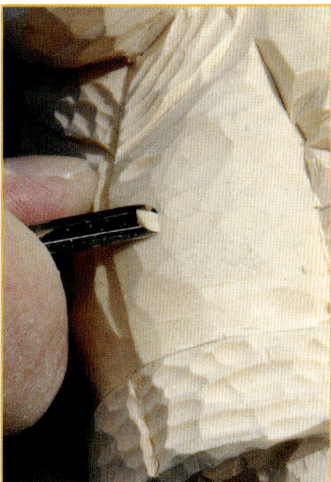 

The result.

The same tool makes indentations for the button and stress pulls on the other side of the coat opening.

Use an eyepunch to form the buttons.

Small knife slices make the button holes.

The result

I'm going to turn my attention to the beard. At this point you can decide between two styles: leaving the knife cuts for a folksy look or finishing it up to show more detail.

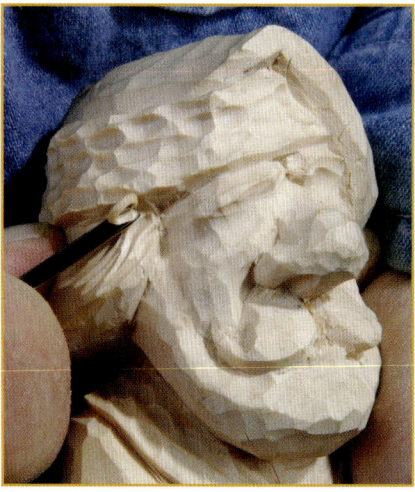
Use a small v-tool or veiner to make the hair lines. The veiner will give a softer look, the v-tool more crisp, which is what I want here to give contrast to the fur trim.

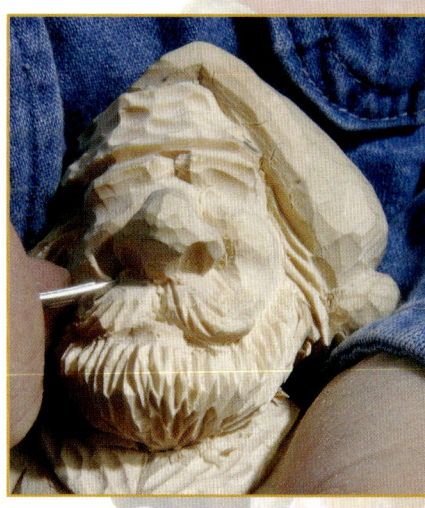
At the moustache, curve the cut to give the natural flow to the hair.

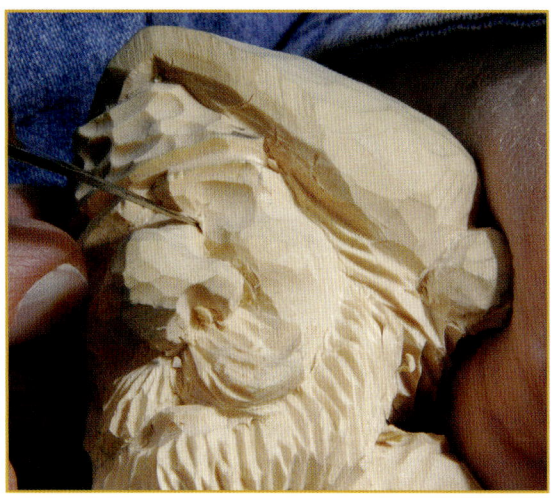
In the inside corner of the eye, cut a deep triangle using three stab cuts…one…

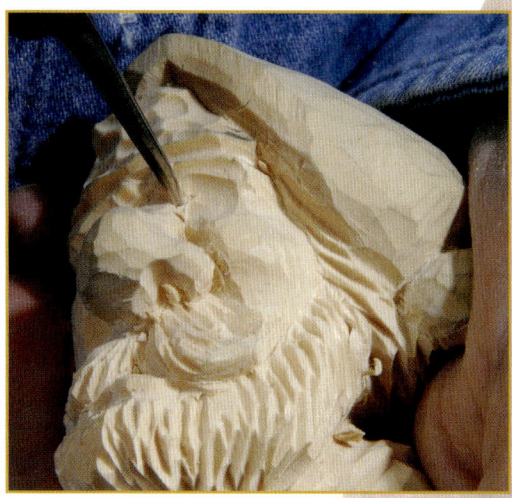
…two…

…three. This deep cut gives more roundness to the eye ball and fights against the common tendency to place the eyes too close together.

The left eye is a little lifted, so I'm run across the eyelid with v-tool to accentuate it.

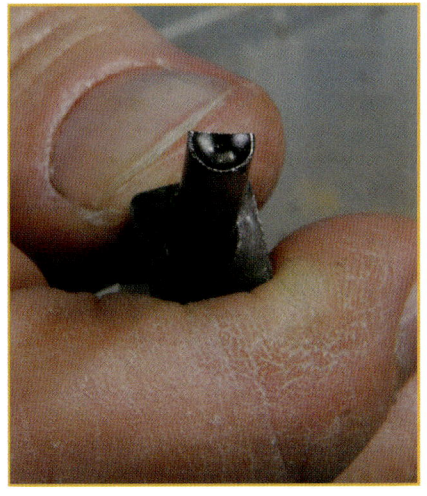

The eyepunch I am using has one edge ground flat. On the raised eye I'll put the round side up and on the other it will be down, the normal position. The larger eyepunch creates the eyeball itself

Position the eyepunch and rock it slightly back and forth with moderate pressure. Flat side up.

Flat side down

The result

The iris uses a smaller ground eyepunch. Both irises will be make with the flat side up.

The result.

Use three cuts in the inside corners of the eyes to deepen them.

Use a double cut to carve a triangle at the outside corner of the eye, giving it a lot more depth. Cut down..

...then up. If it doesn't pop out come at it from the eyeball.

Run a v-tool under the lower eyelid, working from the middle in…

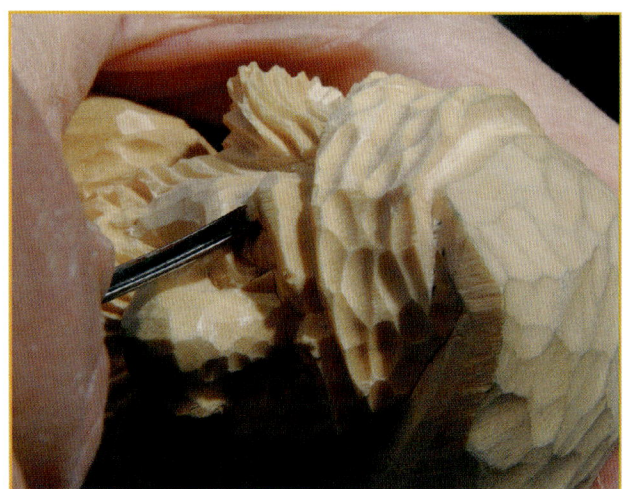
...and the middle out.

The result. These details add a lot of character.

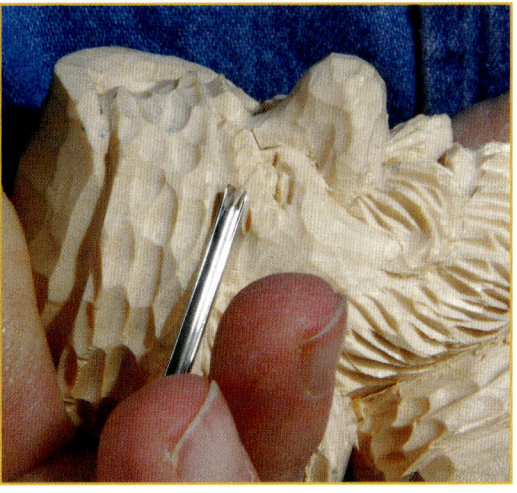

Use the v-tool for the eyebrow hair. The v-tool should be real sharp for this. If it isn't, it just kind of fuzzes it up instead of giving clean cuts. Cut one way, then come back in the opposite direction and nip it off.

He's not looking old enough so I'll add one bag under his eye with the v-tool. Each bag adds 20 years!!!

When we thinned the face we lost some of the cheek detail. I always look for this at the end of a carving because it happens a lot. Use a gouge to take away from the cheek and bring out the cheek bone.

Face detail.

Santa has to have soul….uh, sole. Use a v-tool to create the separation between the soles and the uppers of the boots.

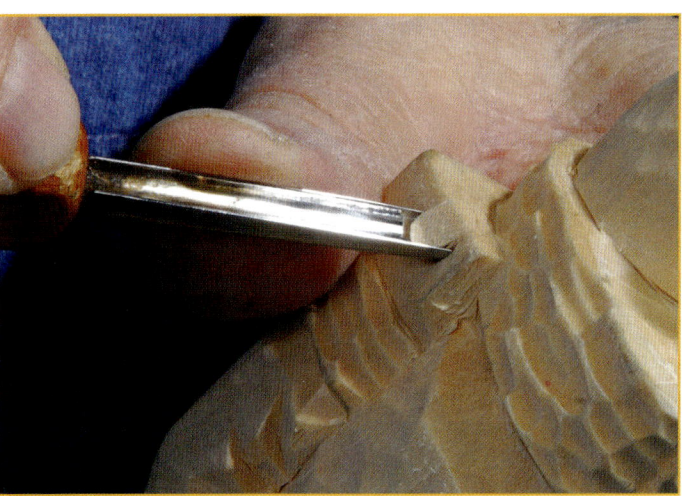

Moving to the mittens, create the thumb making a deep cut with a #9 gouge.

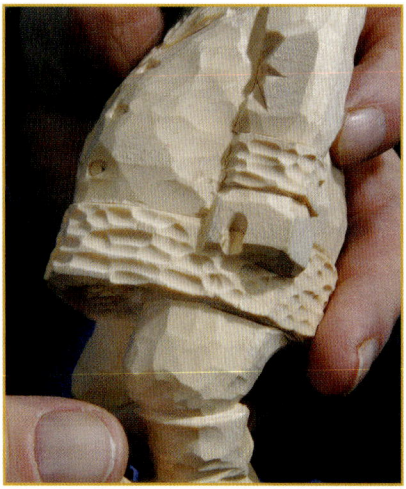
The result.

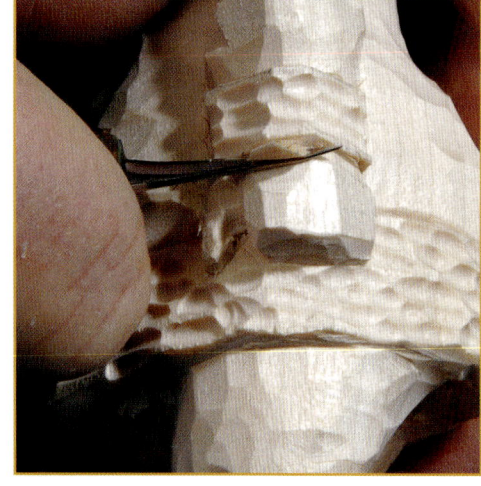
Shape the mitten.

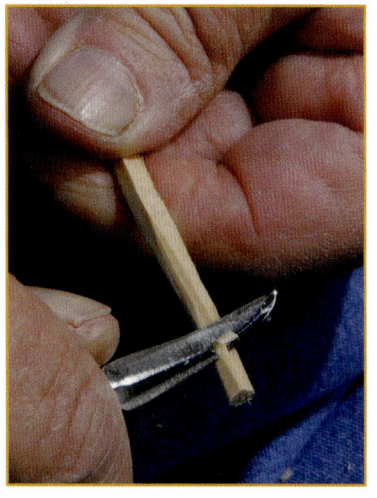
You can add interest by accessorizing your carving. This walkingstick will give him something to do with his hand.

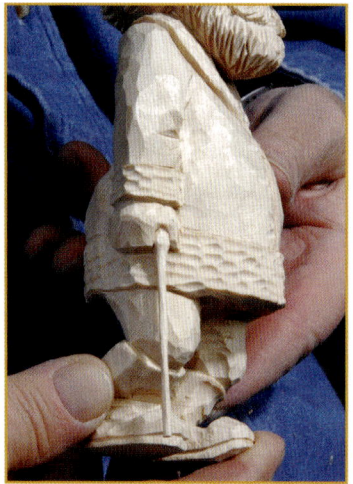
Fit it to the gap between the thumb and fingers, and glue it in place.

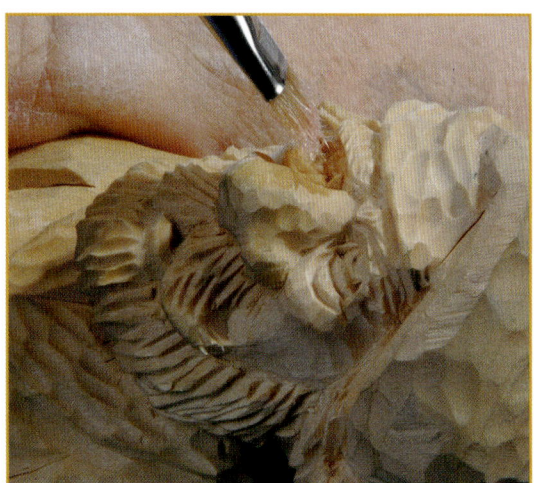
I am using a new way of coloring the faces. "Multichrome" pencils from General Pencil Company work well with turpentine. I give them a good, sharp point and dip them in turpentine. The carving is painted in turpentine before applying the color. This brings out the natural color of the turpentine.

The red is a blend of carmine and scarlet reds. The carmine is used on the lips...

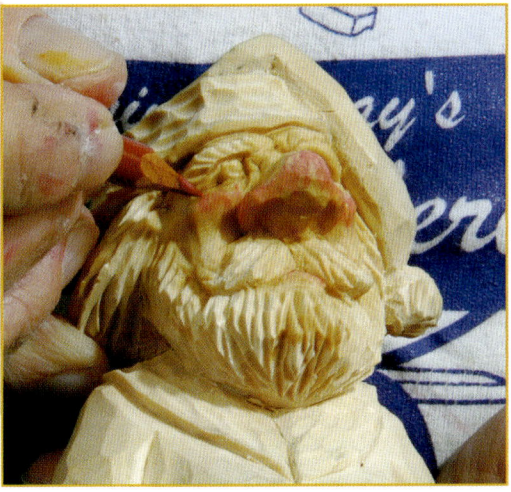
...and the nose and cheeks.

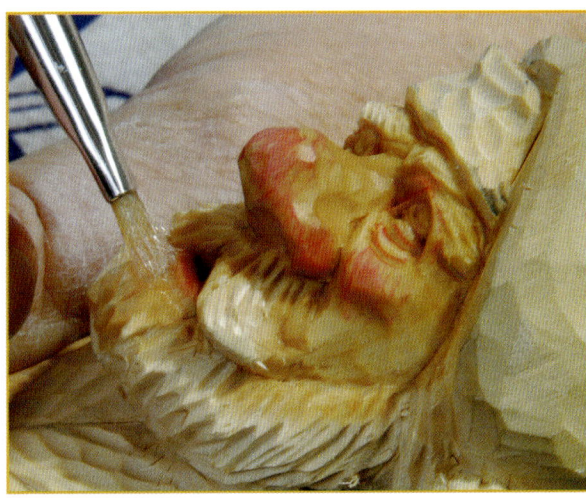
This is blended in with a turpentine brush. It kind of gives the flesh tone.

Progress

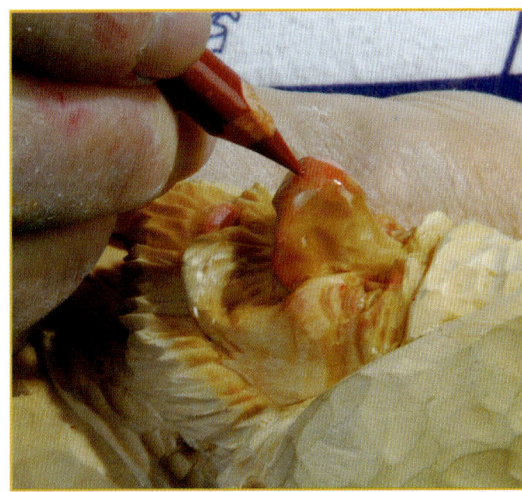
Blush tones are then added with the darker scarlet red.

Blend this in too.

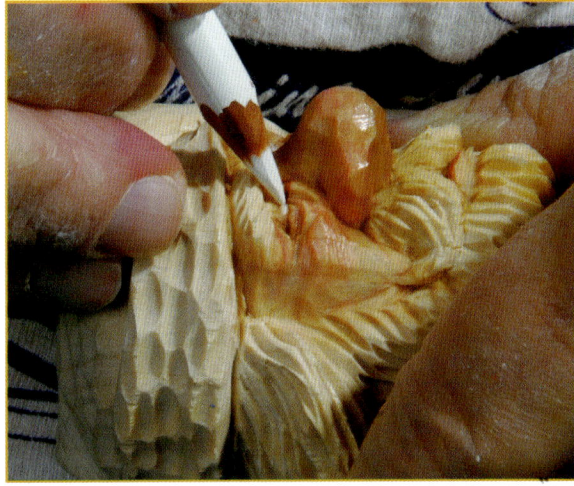
The white of the eyes is done in the same way with a white pencil.

A dark blue is applied to the edge of the iris to bring it out.

The iris is done in a lighter blue.

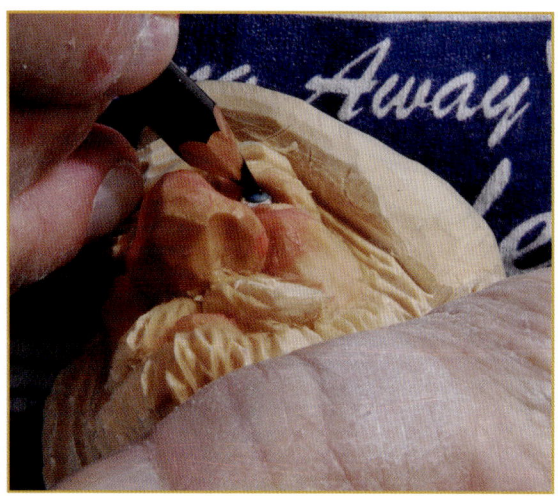
Apply black pencil to the pupil.

The result.

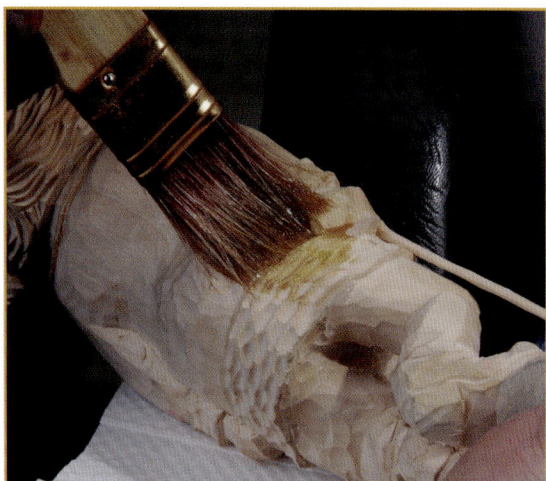
Now paint the figure with linseed oil. This will help in the application of color. Apply a liberal amount and wipe off the excess. I often just dip the piece.

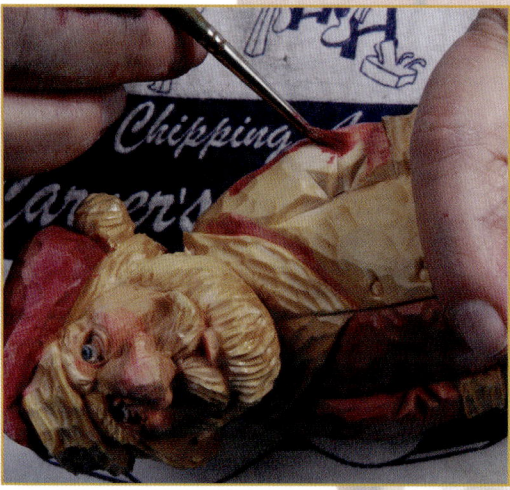
"Santa Claus red" is used for the outfit. I like a oil paint diluted with turpentine. I start with the cap, doing the edges first. This helps guard against the color migrating into the white. Continue with the coat…

...and the pants.

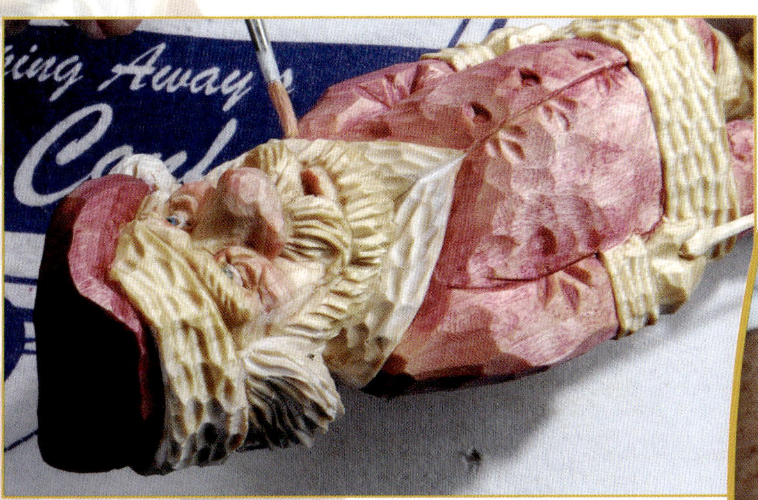

Next paint white on the hair and fur.

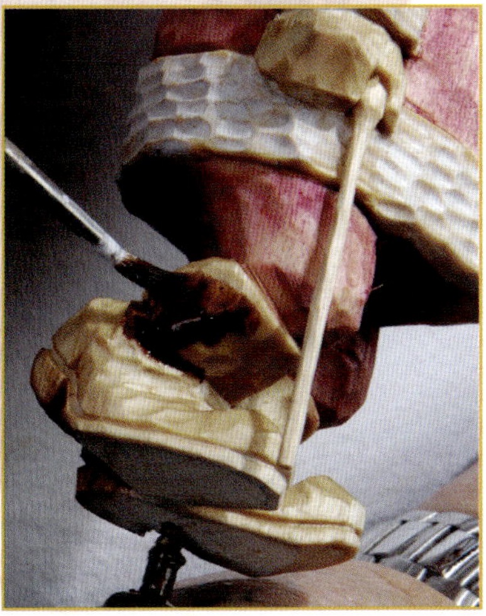

Burnt umber is used on the boots, buttons, and mittens.

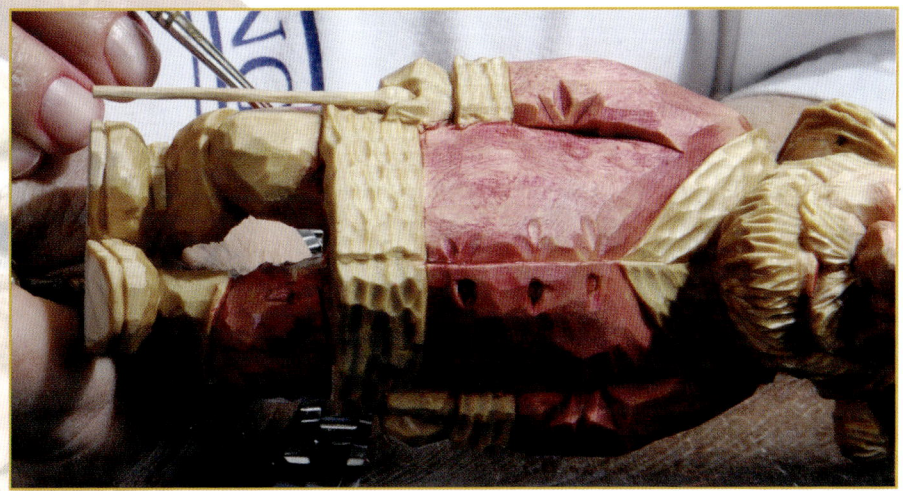

Our Santa is finished.

Gallery

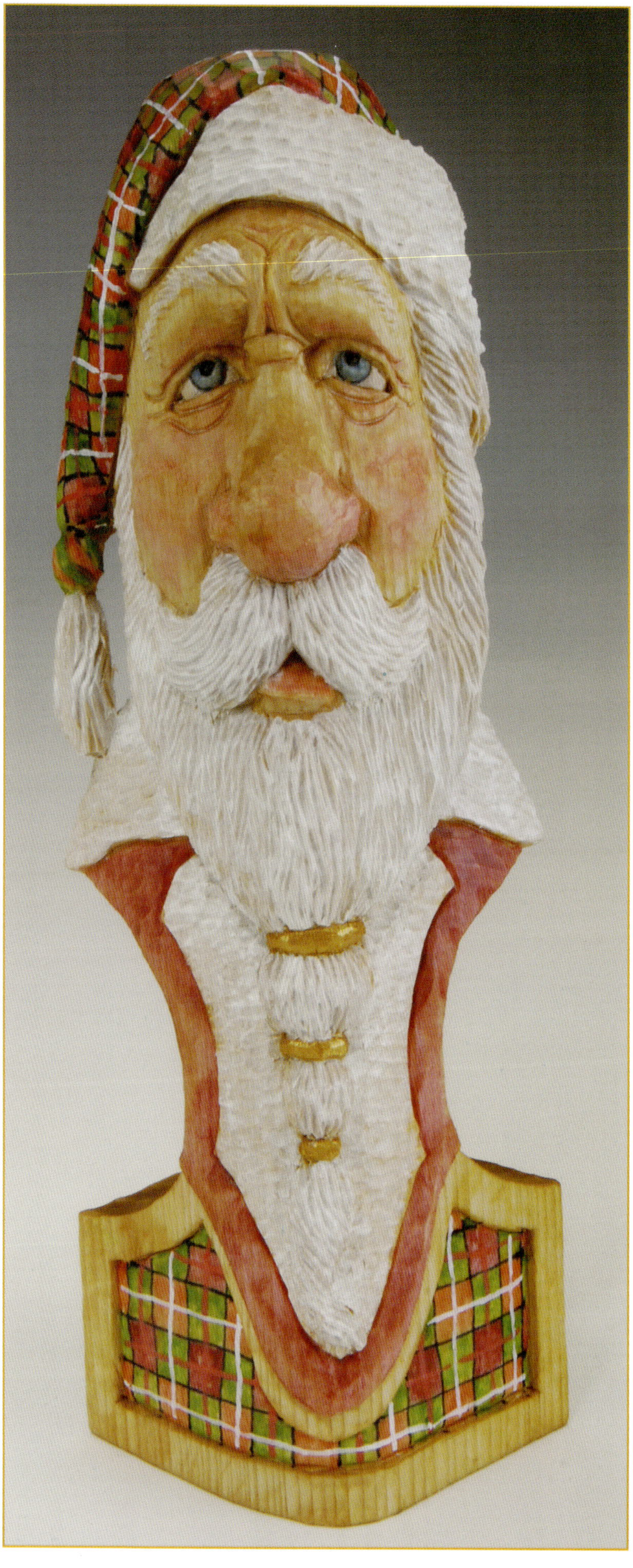